herbertantoniusweiler.de

Herbert Weiler

Of the Hundred and fifty-three fish

Identity and enowning in the image of a number
On a hidden relationship between the writings of John and the three other Gospels

Translation: Birgit Herbst / Herbert Weiler

Cover design: Herbert Weiler

Bibliographic information of the Deutsche Nationalbibliothek:
The Deutsche Nationalbibliothek lists this publication in the
Deutsche Nationalbibliografie; Detailed bibliographic data are
available on the Internet at http://dnb.dnb.de.

© 2018 Herbert Antonius Weiler

Production and publishing: BoD - Books on Demand,
Norderstedt

ISBN 9783752850093

Contents

Notes

Introduction

The number always touched in its explicit nomination, in which it stands alone. The amount of fish was so large that the disciples could not pull the net into the boat but had to drag it to the bank and bring it ashore.

There were 153 big fish. No further hint. The number is mentioned without another narrative context, without numerical relations as it occurs with other figures. The feeding of the five thousand people, for instance, who had followed Jesus without provisions into the desert and who, as it is told, were filled by five breads and two fish, so that still twelve baskets were left over.

Here are just the hundred and fifty-three fish, a number that is specifically mentioned without a following context.

More than other biblical namings of numbers, this seems to be a statement. Only in the writings of John does it occur.

The text of John also differs in other respects from those of the other three evangelists. The prologue, the structural expression, as in the seven *I am*-words of Jesus, as well as the repeated self-denomination of Jesus as the Son of God, are of a philosophical conciseness that distinguishes it from the other three texts.

The juxtapposition of the philosophical dimension of the Gospel of John was already the subject of early scripture interpretation.
The relation of the four Gospels to each other was seen in correspondence with the image of the four living creatures at the throne of God from the vision of Ezekiel and in the revelation of John: Matthew the Angel or Man, Mark the Lion, Luke the Bull, and John the Eagle. Here in accordance with the Aristotelian four reasons of being, the four causalities: the *causa materialis*, the material cause in the symbol of the bull, the *causa formalis*, the form-creating ground or formal cause in the symbol of the lion, the *causa efficiens*, the confronting, encountering or efficient cause in the symbol of the eagle

and the *causa finalis*, the obtaining, final cause in the symbol of the angel or man.
(*The four-quadrants* / Wolfgang Döbereiner)

The eagle assigned to John, symbol of the effecting cause, illustrates the elevation to the opposing, abstract thinking, which has become independent of the sensitivities and conditions of the subjective, and *which rises like an eagle*. Thomas of Aquin

Thus, the different characters of the Gospels in the image of the *Taurus*, the *Lion*, the *Eagle* and the *Angel* are presented as a structure whose elements are interrelated.
Here it is noticeable that the description of the miraculous catch of fish in the days after resurrection, with a peculiar mention of the number of the hundred and fifty-three fish, does not appear in the texts of the other three evangelists.

However, a story which is found among the other evangelists, but not John, is that of the rich man who asks Jesus about the acquisition of the Kingdom of Heaven, ending with the well-known parable of the camel and the eye of the needle.

It occurs almost identically in Mark, Luke and Matthew.

Considering the etymological context of the words in the Hebrew language and the traditional numerical and pictorial meaning of the Hebrew letters, a hidden correspondence between the three other Gospels and that of John becomes apparent.

Simon Peter went up and drew the net to land, full of large fish, a hundred and fifty-three; and although there were so many, the net was not torn.
John, 21,11

Of the Hundred and Fifty-Three Fish

In the days after the Resurrection, as John tells, the disciples put their boat out to Lake Tiberias to fish.

They had not caught anything the whole night, and when it was morning they returned to the shore. There stood Jesus but they did not recognize him.

His question whether they have something to eat, they can only deny.

He advises them to go out again and throw out the net on the right side of the boat.

They do as he says, and then the net is so full that they can no longer pull it into the boat but have to drag it ashore.

Then Peter realizes that it is Christ. He jumps into the water to reach the shore faster.

The net, it is stated later, was filled with one hundred and fifty-three large fish, and though there were so many, it did not tear.

This story of the catch of fish at night with mention of the hundred and fifty-three fish is found only in the gospel of John.

The number seventeen

Augustine, the christian theologican and philosopher gave much thought to the meaning of the number. He named the seventeen as one of its keys.
The practice of ancient numerical theories involved looking at numbers in proportion to the sum resulting from the addition of their series.
A sentence ascribed to Pythagoras illustrates this relation: *What you think is four is ten.*
The addition of the four, one plus two plus three plus four, yields ten.
Augustine applied this practice to the hundred and fifty-three: *counting from one to seventeen and adding all the intervening numbers adds up to one hundred and three and fifty,* he explained in response to the questions of his pupil Januarius (XXXIII Answer to the Questions of Januarius, 2. book.)

Augustine considered the *Seventeen* as a perfect figure because it contains the number of the Ten Commandments and that of the seven gifts of the Holy Spirit. Thomas Aquinas shared this interpretation.

In the seventeen, the sum of ten as the number of the earthly - ten commandments for earthly life - and the seven as number of heaven - seven days of creation, seven gifts of the Holy Spirit - Thomas saw a reference to the descent of the celestial to earth, to the incarnation of Christ.

Consequently, in the hundred and fifty-three as an addition of the Seventeen, after Easter, the completion of the incarnation of is expressed.

A reference to what happened on Pentecost is made in the Book of Acts. Here seventeen language groups are mentioned after the Holy Spirit had descended upon the congregation and they could speak in foreign dialects.

In the tradition of Christianity, therefore, the number of hundred and fifty-three fish, with the previous call from now on to become fishers of men, is understood as an indication that the Christian message should be carried to all peoples.

The Seventeen is often mentioned in the Old Testament.

On the seventeenth day of the second month, the Flood began, and on the seventeenth day of the seventh month, Noah's Ark sat on Mount Ararat.
Joseph was seventeen years old when his brothers sold him to Egypt; Jacob lived in Egypt for another seventeen years.
Ten times the Seventeen is mentioned in the Tanach - in the New Testament it does not appear as a number. Here reference is only made to the 153, the number of its addition series.

The number of fish in John, however, holds another statement that goes beyond its mathematical structure in the context of the Seventeen.

Word, Number and Image

In Hebrew, the numbers are represented by the characters of the letter sequence. The series of the ones with the first nine letters, the series of the tens with the following nine letters and the series of the hundreds with the remaining four characters.

The sequence of the twenty-two letters of theHebrew alphabet ends with the letter *thaw* which stands for the four hundred:

9	8	7	6	5	4	3	2	1
ט	ח	ז	ו	ה	ד	ג	ב	א
tet	khet	zayin	vaw	he	dalet	gimel	bet	aleph
uterus	fence	sword	hook	window	door	camel	house	bull's head

70	60	50	40	30	20	10
ע	ס	נ	מ	ל	כ	י
ayin	samekh	nun	mem	lamed	kaf	yod
eye	snake	fish	water	ox sting	palm	hand

400	300	200	100	90	80
ת	ש	ר	ק	צ	פ
tav	shin	resh	qof	tzadi	phe
cross. sign	teeth	head	eye of the needle	fishhook	mouth

Thus, a word can yield a number and a number can be read as a word. Identical numerical values are interpreted in a specific form of the Jewish text-interpretation, the Gematria, as indication of a context. This approach to the biblical writings by means of the numerical value of Hebrew words evolved to a common system in post-biblical Judaism.

Despite the distance of some Judaist teachers, including Maimonides, who rejected the Gematria because of the possibility of speculative arbitrariness, this form of scriptural interpretation is an integral part of Jewish mysticism, the Kabbalah.
Christian humanists in dialogue with teachers of Judaism saw in the Gematria, as in the Kabbalah in general, a way to a deeper understanding of the Christian texts.
Known here are Flavius Mithridates, a Christian convert, his pupil Pico della Mirandola, Johannes Reuchlin and Agrippa von Nettesheim.

A speculative arbitrariness notwithstanding, in the case of such a peculiar numerical indication as in the citation of the hundred and fifty-three fish, it seems obvious to pursue the correspondence between number and word.

All the more so, since in regard to a different number, namely in the *Revelation of John*, it is explicitly recommended to consider the importance of a number.

Here is wisdom. Let him that has understanding count the number of the beast: for it is the number of a man; and his number is Six hundred three score and six.
Rev.13:18

In any case, it will be understandable that in a language in which the numbers are represented by letters, the relationship between numerical value and character is naturally and more directly present than in a language using separate numerals.

For example, the number 17, which is linked to the miraculous catch of fish by Augustin and Thomas, is found in the Hebrew word for *good* - טוב - *tov*.

This word consists of the letters *Tet* - ט, *vav* - ו and *Bet* - ב.

Tet means nine, *Vaw* equals six and *Bet* two. The numerical value of the letters adds up to seventeen.

The word is mentioned seven times right at the beginning of Genesis, in the sentence: *And God saw that it was good.*

Considering the Hebrew numbers representing the *hundred and fifty-three* in this way, it consists of the letters *Kuph* – ק , for *hundred*, *Nun* נ , for *fifty* and *Gimel* – ג , for *three.*
At the time of the creation of the Gospels and also in modern Hebrew, the number 153 is written in the following way: קנג

In the tradition of the Hebrew alphabet, however, each letter is - apart from its numerical value - associated with a metaphorical meaning, a picture (see illustration), which historically derives from an earlier, still figurative form of the characters.
This meaning is not unknown or hidden in present-day Hebrew usage but rather generally present, since many of the letter names are identical or etymologically similar to the commonly used terms, such as in the case of *house, eye, door* or *teeth.*

Thus, the letter *bet* - ב, to which the numerical value 2 belongs, is called *house*, as is the common Hebrew word for *house*.

The letter *gimel-* ג, corresponding to the numerical value 3, is called *camel*, whose name in present-day Hebrew is *gamal,* written just like the name of the letter - גמל – *gml.*

Looking at the numerals of the *hundred and fifty-three* in this way, the sign for the Hundred, *kuph-*ק , means a *needle eye*, the sign for the *fifty*, *nun-* נ means *fish* and the sign of the *three*, *gimel-* ג, is called *camel*.
Thus, in the Hebrew representation of the number 153 – read in Hebrew order from right to left – we find included the images *eye of a needle, fish* and *camel-* קנג.

The *camel* and the *eye of the needle* are well-known from the other three of the Evangelists. Their connection has become proverbial.
Only in this way, in the form of numbers, they also appear in the Gospel of John, which otherwise does not mention the parable.

Before they mention the camel and the eye of the needle, Mark, Luke and Matthew tell the story of the rich young man.
The man, whom Luke calls a certain leader, approaches Jesus and asks him: *Good Master, what shall I do to inherit eternal life?*
Jesus answers: *What do you call me good, no one is good except God alone*, and he refers him to the commandments.

In Matthew, the man asks, *Master, what good must I do to have eternal life?*
And Jesus answers here, *What do you ask me about what is good. Good is only one. But if you want to enter into life, follow the commandments.*

Common to all three accounts is the triple mention of the word *good*, once by the man, contained in the question, and twice in the answer of Jesus.
The man then asks what he is still lacking since he has obeyed the commandments from his youth.
Thereupon, as it is said, Jesus grows fond of him, and tells him:

One thing is missing, go and sell everything you have, and give it to the poor, so you will have a treasure in heaven, and come, follow me.
Sadly the young man went away because he had great possessions.
Then Jesus turned to his disciples and said: *It is hard for a rich man to enter into the kingdom of heaven. It is easier for a camel to go through the eye of a needle than for a rich man to enter the kingdom of God.*

It is reported that the disciples were very shocked.
They were fishermen, probably sharing a common net and boat and not to be called rich. Why are they so concerned?

According to Romano Guardini, who emphasizes this conversation, it seems that they refer Jesus' statement to every person and his relationship to all possessions, because they ask:
Then who can be saved at all?
How can anyone ever own something and not be determined by it?
Jesus answers: *What is impossible with men, that is possible with God.*

If, on the basis of the number of the 153 fish in John, a hidden relation to the parable of the camel and the eye of the needle opens for the three other evangelists, in Matthew, Mark and Luke in the story of the rich man, which takes place long before Easter, something seems to be addressed that after Easter at John 21, in the story of the night of fishing, again finds an answer.

In contrast to the mention in the three other Gospels, here, in this form of naming the number 153, the *nun* - נ - the *fish* is added to the camel and the eye of the needle.
It seems that now, after the Resurrection, something has changed in the relationship between the camel and the eye of the needle, as if something had been added. And that which has been added is expressed by the *fish*.

The Fish – the *Nun*

The early Christians associated the image
of the fish with Christ. In the Greek word
for *fish*, *ICHTHYS,* they recognized the
initials of the words *Iesous Christos
Theou Yios Soter - Jesus Christ, Son of
God, Savior.*
Therefore, Tertullian speaks of Christ as a
fish, from which the little fish, the
Christians, emerge.
Wulfila, who for the first time translated
the Bible from Greek into a Germanic
language, namely into Gothic, and
developed a script specifically for it,
formed from the initials of *Iesous
Christos*, the fundamental Germanic word
of identity – *I.CH.*

However, the connection of the figure of
the Messiah with the picture of the single
fish from which the fish originate is older
and has been present before; it derived
from the meaning of the fish in the
Gospels as well as from the blessing of
Jacob on his grandchildren:: *They shall be
like the fish.* Gen. 48,16

In rabbinic Judaism, water was the image of the Torah and the fish was the parable of Israel.

Although in the Hebrew tradition the letter *Nun* - נון is associated with the image of the fish, the word *Dag* - דג is usually used in the Bible.
The name *Nun* was the common word in Aramaic.
As designation for the fish it could be found, equally or similarly sounding, in the whole Semitic language area.
In Babylonia and Assyria it formed a part of several names of gods, persons, and places, dating back to the Sumerian, where it referred to divine sponsorship, similar to the syllable *el* later on.

In neighbouring Egypt *Nun* was the name of the prime Egyptian god, who was understood as the Lord of the primeval waters, before the very beginning. As the only god of the Egyptian pantheon he was imagined as being of pure human form. The primordial God *Nun,* in the view of the Egyptians, was connected with the annual Nile flood.

In the flood and retreat of the water at the end of the inundation, when the emerging, once dry land sprouted new life, the Egyptians saw a picture of the work of *Nun*.

The fish, in whose belly Jonah spends three days, in the book Jonah is called *dag gadol*, a *big fish,* while in Arabic it is called *al nun*. Jonah who also bears the epithet *dhun nun*, the *master of the fish*. Likewise the city of *Ninive* - נִינְוֵה, with whose fate that of Jonah is linked, contains the *Nun* in its name.

Apart from that in the Old Testament fish, fishing and fishing are mentioned only rarely.

In the New Testament, on the other hand, they are a recurrent theme.

For instance, the disciples are professional fishermen; in the feeding of the five thousand it is bread and fish that are multiplied; after the resurrection Jesus appears to the disciples and they give him *a piece of broiled fish with a honey-pie;* Jesus instructs the disciples, from now on to be *human fishermen*, and in John's Gospel there is the story of the miraculous catch of fish.

In the Old Testament, however, the word *Nun* appears in a very distinctive context. *Yehoshua*, the disciple and servant of Moses, who, after his death, leads the people into the Promised Land, is called *Yehoshua, Son of Nun* after the proclamation at Sinai, where he had accompanied Moses up the mountain.

This *Nun* himself, the father of Yehoshua, does not appear.
However, from the time of the Proclamation on Mount Sinai to the crossing of the Jordan, he is referred to in every mention of Jehoshua; afterwards several more times, and the last time at the death of Yehoshua.
Yehoshua - יהושע means: *The Lord saves*. *Jesus - Yeshua*, in addition to *Joshua,* represents the other Latinized short form of the name. Therefore, at the announcement of the pregnancy of Mary, the angel speaks to Joseph: *She will give birth to a son, and you are to give him the name Jesus, because he will save his people from their sins.* Matt 1,21

Yehoshua, son of Nun, is the one who leads the people into the Promised Land after forty years of desert migration. What is obvious here is that the number *forty* corresponds to the letter *Mem* - מ, which means *water*.

The *Nun* - נ - on the other hand, the *fifty* - the *fish* - represents what lives in the water, what comes out of the water, what is given by the water, the *fruits of the sea*, as it is said in Genesis.

The fourty years of walking through the wilderness, after four hundred years of Egyptian captivity, began with passing through the divided waters of the Red Sea and ended with the crossing of the waters of the Jordan and reaching the Promised Land. During the migration, the people received the Torah.

The *Nun* is the result, the sense of waiting - the *fifty* follows the *forty.*

Mem - מ, the *forty,* the *water,* as well as the *four, Dalet* - ד, the *door,* and the *four hundred*, *Taw* - ת, the *cross*, bear a reference to the time.

There are certain periods of time in the Bible that are measured forty and four hundred, respectively:

The forty years of wandering through the desert; the forty days of the Sinai; the four hundred years in exile; forty days that Jesus fasted in the desert; four days Lazarus had already been buried in the tomb when Jesus raised him from the dead.

These periods of time are characterized by the fact that they are faced with a new beginning.

After the four hundred years in Egypt, the Israelites emerge as a people for the first time. After the forty days on Sinai, they receive the Torah, after forty years in the desert they reach the Promised Land.

The Hebrew letter *Nun* - נ, the *fish*, sign for the *fifty*, follows the *Mem* - מ, sign for *forty*, which stands for the *water*.

The immanence of the Fifth in the Four is also present in the four directions, front, back, right and left, corresponding to the four cardinal points, the fifth element of which is the centre point, the subject.

Conversely, the given quadrangle
represents the first geometric figure,
which opens up a fifth point without
further assistance, solely by drawing the
diagonals.
The concept of time to which *Mem* מ
refers is like the water in which nothing is
yet tangible. A time before the beginning.
It is the waiting.

The Beginning

It is the water that conveys the experience
of the intangible. It touches and flows
around the hands, but nothing can be
grasped. It can only be scooped.
It is characterized by presence as well as
by amorphousness.

The fish appears from out of the water. It
can be spotted in the water. It inhabits the
intangible, that which is hardly tangible; it
evaporates, can be grasped only in a net,
when it emerges from the water.

The fish in the water indicates what is still in the undivided waiting. It wants to be present. It is waiting for its beginning.

This opens the meaning of the German word *fangen – to catch* in the word *Anfang - beginning*.
It is related to *Fähigkeit – ability*, deriving from the Middle High German word *fahen*. Originally it means *grasp, make tangible.*

Maybe the German word *Fisch* or English *fish* refers to *fassen - grasping* or *erfassen - com-prehending*, which as an elementary principle can only be articulated in relation to the incomprehensible - the water.
The fish as what comes out of the incomprehensible, intangible.
Principle of the beginning, out of nothingness.

Likewise the astrological sign *Pisces* as beginning of the upper movement of the zodiac, the *path of aphrodite* (W. Döbereiner) from the sign *Pisces*, the inherent, to the sign *Libra*, the presence.

The *fifty*, the *Nun*, means *beginning*.
Thus, according to the Torah, after a
period of 49 years in the fiftieth year, the
so called *jobel-year*, it came to a general
new beginning of economic life. Man
should be freed from all dependencies and
be able to start afresh.

This happened with the return of all
acquired possessions to their original
owners.
In Judaism, on the fiftieth day after the
beginning of Passover, *Shavuoth* is
celebrated, the feast of the giving of the
Torah at the Sinai.
Thus, according to the significance of the
festival in the Jewish tradition, for the first
time each individual was personally
addressed by God.

In contrast to the collectivist cultures of
priesthood and divine kingship, as e.g. in
Egypt and among the other peoples, God
applies the Torah to the individual, who
henceforth has a personal relationship to
Him, independent from the collective.
It was the feast of *Shavuot* to which the
disciples of Jesus had gathered when the

Holy Spirit descended on each one of them.
This event then became Pentecost for the Christians.

(*Pentecost,* from Greek *Pente cost = fifty*).

To have an own spirit means to have an own beginning (Romano Guardin), to enter into a relationship out of one's own motion.

Therefore, in Jewish mysticism, the letter *Nun* and its number, the *fifty,* are associated with individuation.

The blessing of Jacob on his grandchildren Ephraim and Manasseh, Gen. 48,16 that *they shall multiply in the midst of the land like the fish,* here finds its essential interpretation.
The fish, coming out of the water, bringing the not yet tangible to the beginning, represents the principle of becoming.
What *is* not yet, is given existence by the fish, it emerges, becomes a being.

The *fish* is the mediation, the relationship inherent in existence.

The basic statement of existence is: *I am* or *thou are* or *it is*.
The statement contains two elements: the naming of beings, *thou, I* or *It*, and the naming of the being of beings, that it *is*.

It is a result of the Greek thinking that the being of that what *i*s addressed finds its expression in the language, and that the addressed thereby receives a presence, separate from the subject, opposite to it, object of thinking.

The *fish* represents the relationship, the pivot of the two limbs of existence.
The Hebrew word השמים - *haSchamaim,* which is commonly translated with *heaven* in Genesis, literally means *the waters there.*
The *Nun* comes from *the waters there.* It is the beginning of being out of nothingness.

Heidegger calls the relationship of the two members to each other the *Ereignis* – con-cern, *occurence* or *enowning.* The German term *Ereignis* usually translated as *an event*, comes from the German prefix, *er-*, meaning a move away from

subject, towards an opening, and *Auge,
eye*. understood in terms of something
coming into view, German *eräugen*. An
approximate translation renders the word
as *enowning*; that in connection with
things that arise and appear, that they are
arising *into their own*. K. Maly / P. Emad
In the *enownig*, according to Heidegger,
the two limbs of existence have *enowned*
each other *coming into themselves by
belonging together.* H. Dreyfus

The enowning is like the knee through
which the movement of the above
communicates with the lower

The knee forms the joint, the pivot,
between upper and lower leg.
It is the hub of the moving and the being
moved.
Just as the middle, the separation of wax
and stamp, allows for the print, and
contains the meaning of wax and seal, the
meaning of the limbs is the movement.
The knee as an expression of one's own
movement. This explains the etymological
relationship of the Indo-European *knee -
genu* and *fathering, birth* or *sex* (gen).
The Greek concepts of *Genesis*, of

creation, as well as *Kinesis*, belong in this etymological context.

It was customary among the Germanic tribes for the father to welcome his new born child and bless him by putting him on his knee.

Similarly, in Hebrew, where the word for *knee - berech -* ברך, and the word for *blessing, bracha -* ברכה, have the same root.

Joseph Beuys commented on this context with the remark: *In any case, I think with my knee! Ich denke sowieso mit dem Knie*

Would this pivotal point between the entities and the being, between *I, you, he, she, it,* and *am, are, is* speak to us and express itself, it would say:
I am the principle of being, above all beings' I am the I am'. I am the identity, the presence of presentness.

This is the name that God announces to Moses from out of the burning bush. Identity consists in expenditure. That's the *en-owning*. It is *the burning bush that does not burn*.

The continuity of the Same in the identity in Greek philosophy is described with the concept of *ousia* - οὐσία, the *essence* or *essential*.

The fact that within the languages of Greco-Roman cultural area it is possible to name the *being*, the *is-ness* of things - that *is* this - is an inheritance of Greek philosophy, in which one began to recognize and articulate the essence of things in their appearance.

As something that exists, as in any drinking glass, as the essential of a drinking glass.

When we say *this is a cup*, we actually use a verb to express that the essence - *Wesen* of the cup becomes present. *This is a cup* means: *This essences a cup.*

We articulate a work. The essence of the cup *works* in the cup. Or *works* the cup.

The scholastics debated the question of whether *in*, *before* or *behind* things in the dispute of universalia.

We are actually saying that in this the *Wesen* - essence of a cup is present. Because the essence of things, by being present, signifies the permanence of things, the concept of *ousia* in Greek has also been associated with the durability of existence and, as such, also with possession.

Similarly, in German, when they speak of an *Anwesen - estate*.
It forms a philological connection to the meaning of *Eigentliches* or *Eigentümliches,* coming from the adjective *eigen – own,* which means the peculiarity of something, its character.

In the sign of Aquarius the essence emerges from the still undivided essence of the sign Pisces and becomes the polarity of I and thou. In the lower movement, from Aries to Taurus, it results in the limitation and permanence of things. (W. Döbereiner)

The identity of the essence becomes the continuity of its appearance.

In the phase of Aquarius, the person of man comes to the beginning.
Therefore, in the tetramorph of the Prophet's vision, Aquarius is also depicted as a human or an angel. In the old

depictions, next to the heads of Taurus, Leo and Eagle, a human face looks out of the picture for Aquarius.

It is always the Aquarians who articulate the topic of polarity: Martin Buber with *I and Thou*, the *Dialogic Principle*, Romano Guardini with the definition of the person about his own beginning and the principle of opposite. Or Ilya Prigogine, who in his criticism of a deterministic natural science recommends recognizing nature as a dialogical counterpart and demands a *dialogue with nature*.

Identity, from the Latin word *idem - the same* - means that something is *itself the same*. sich selbst das Selbe (Martin Heidegger)
That is the *ousia*, the essence.
Identity arises in Aquarius. In the opposite movement, in the phase of Taurus, it becomes appearance, in the permanence of the same in appearance.

Why *itself the same*?
Because otherwise it would only be the identifiability of properties, *itself the same,* however, designates the subject of the properties.

That is the thing about a cup.
It comes to itself when its essence is being
recognized by man.
The Aristotelian theorem of identity, *A is
A*, thus means that *A* becomes *A* by the
essence of A becoming present:
The table is a table because the essence of
the table, what all the tables have in
common, becomes present in it.

In the presence of man the essence of
things can become present, according to
Master Ekkehard.

This is the fish that is included in the
number of the miraculous catch of fish.
Man is human because he has his own
Nun.
He can say: *I am*. Only he can make that
statement.
Although all people have this in common,
only each individual person can make that
statement of himself or herself.
In the *Burning Bush* it is the identity itself
that enowns - becomes an enowning

Therefore, in Hebrew, the word for human
or person, *anosch*, is based on the root *ani*
that means *I.*

Man is the one who can say *I*.
So the nocturnal fishing trip is also the
sleep from which man wakes up in the
morning, comes back to the shore and,
although he was not present during sleep,
he is the same again. The fish is what he
brings along from his nocturnal sea of
sleep.

The Babylonian astrologer Berossos
speaks of a divine saviour who rises every
morning at the same time in the form of a
man and a fish from the sea, to instruct
the people regarding the foundations of
culture, agriculture, architecture, writing
and all the arts.
In the evening he returns into the sea.

The possibility of naming the *ousia*,
the *is-ness* of things, implies that they are
juxtaposed as otherness.
This is thinking as recognizing the
essence in the encounter.
Identity means to be in relationship.
Identifying identity is possible because
the principle of relationship could be
internalized: the *I-Thou* (Martin Buber).
Jesus says: *I am the door.* (John 10:9)

It is the identity of man that enables him to be a person and to recognize the identity in things.

Identity is always the identity of the individual human being. Namely, by being himself the same. And what he recognizes as the same can be the same in it.

In the recognizing of man, the essence of things can be present -

By seeing the things, you bring them back to God. Look what you all do, says Master Ekkehard.

Here is a way of understanding the naming of the 153 fish in the Book of John of the miraculous fish-catch after the resurrection.

And why in the number of fish *Nun - the fish*, between camel and needle eye is mentioned.

The enowning The anarchist principle

The enowning, the occurence of the Incarnation can be understood as the occurence par excellence. When Christ became man, he enowned himself. This allowed for the ability of enowning - the person-being of man.

The life of the individual as a biography previously had no meaning. The individual person was previously not able to occur, to enown; his fate was the fate of his clan, his people.
When the Torah was proclaimed on Sinai, for the first time man was addressed as an individual with a personal relationship to God.
Later the prophet Jeremiah hinted at the independence from external terms, as this relationship would one day be internalized:
I will put my law within them and I will write it on their hearts. ... Then no one will teach his neighbor or his brother and say: Know the LORD: for they shall all know me, from the least of them unto the greatest. (Jer. 31: 34)

Gregory of Nyssa, much revered in the Orthodox Church, categorically formulated this essential anarchism of authority-independent knowledge and encounter with God: *More important than all else is that we are not subjected to any necessity and subservient to any power in bondage; but it is up to us to do what we want and to do. For virtue is a matter of voluntarism and not subjection. What arises from coercion and violence is therefore no virtue.*
(Gregory of Nyssa, de hominis opificio)

Jesus recounts this in the story of the one repentant sinner who is in the decision and, only in repentance finds to his own ethical movement. And, therefore, he is closer to God than the Nine and ninety Righteous. (Luke 15: 9)

Through the Christ-enowning man could become a person.
Whoever drinks of my water becomes the source of living water, says Jesus to the Samaritan woman at the *Well of Sychar.* Through him, every human being is unique and is capable of his own beginning, he is able to act out of his own reason. (R. Guardini)

This is his *Nun*.

After having caught nothing the night before, the disciples are to go out to the lake once again. But now they are supposed to cast their net on the right side of the boat, says Jesus.

A horizontal line seems to be ascending as it goes higher to the right, and seems to be descending as it goes lower to the right.
We locate the beginning of the path on the left, but it leads to the right side.
The right side appears as an open expanse, it forms the space, the opposite.
From the right comes what comes *to* us, what we receive.
To the right goes the direction in which we move, the path of what emanates from us, whose beginning is in us.
Jesus' recommendation to cast the nets on the right side of the boat indicates a change: Man is no longer just the recipient, but he has his own beginning and he enters into encounter.
He now has internalized the *sense destination* that hitherto approached him from the outside.

In the encounter, the awareness of the essence in the Other, man finds the beginning. Here he becomes a person. The mission to become *fisherman of men* is to convey this beginning, the Christ-Enowning, to each human being, so that everyone may bring, what is given to him to the present, to the shore of time, just as Christ, the beginning, himself came into the time.

Camel and eye of a needle

The paradox in the parable of the camel and the eye of a needle has sometimes been interpreted as the result of a mistranslation.
Since the words *Camel-Kamelo*s-Κάμήλος and *Ship's rope - Kamilos*-Κάμίλός were similar in Greek, some believe that the camel had come into the context through a confusion.
Jesus then actually spoke of the rope, which fits through a needle eye rather than a rich man enters the Kingdom of Heaven.

A similar objection refers to an Aramaic word for ship's-rope, *gamta*, which would have been reversed by confusing one letter with *gamal.* (Pinchas Lapide)

To speak of a ship's rope, which was more likely to go through the needle-eye, may have been quite common among the fishermen at the Sea of Galilee.

Since such a saying would undoubtedly have been known to the authors of the Gospels a confusion does not seem very plausible here.

In addition, the described dismay of the disciples rather indicates a more fundamental impossibility, than the gradual difference of a thread enlarged to the rope represents.

In a merely gradual statement of possessions and richness, the question of the apostles as to who could be saved at all - since this also applies to those less rich - would not have made sense.

In any case, one could ask why, when translating a doubtful passage, the absurd version should have been preferred.

Furthermore, such a critique of the traditional form of the parable is already invalidated a few paragraphs later on the basis of a similarly drastic comparison: ... *You blind guides, straining out a gnat, while swallowing a camel!*. (Math. 23, 24)

The mention of camel and eye of the needle in relation to the inability of the rich man to give his possessions to the poor has, however, a greater significance than just that of a rhetorical accentuation. It can be inferred from the etymological transparency of words and phrases that are inherent in the Hebrew language. For instance the word for *camel*, גמל - *gamal*, is the same as the word for *weaning* גמל - *gamal*, such as the baby from the mother 's breast. Equally for *ripening,* as the detachment of the fruit from the stem.

In this respect it is akin to the word for *giving back, repaying* גמל - *gamal*, in the sense of *doing good* or *charity.*

The benefactor who gives to the poor is therefore called גמל דלים - *gomel dalim*, and the word גמילות - *gmiluth* means *charity*.

Since Jesus, in his previous demand to the rich man to to part with his possessions and give them to the poor, presumably used these words, the subsequent emphasis of the camel, *gamal*- גמל, in his address to the disciples has an immediate associative and phonetic reference to the aforementioned charity.

Similarly, that other passage in which he compares the camel with the previous mention of mercy: *you have set aside the essential things of the law: right and mercy and faith. You blind guides, straining out a gnat, while swallowing a camel!*. Math. 23.24

The parable thus takes on the character of a recommendation and goes beyond a mere illustration of disproportionality. In Jewish tradition, the *needle eye* ק - *kuph* - is associated with the entrance into heaven as a numerical symbol for the one hundred, as if it were the entrance into the space of the hundreds.

It is a metaphor for the *narrow path* that is mentioned in the Gospels.
The statement that a *camel - Gamal* passes through the *neelde eye - kuph* rather than a rich man enters the kingdom of heaven turns out to be a hint: Rather someone who is weaned from possession, who is able to give it away and is a benefactor, goes to the kingdom of heaven - as a rich man.

Another level of the word-stem belonging to גמל - *gamal* is found in the word גמול - *gimul* for *deed* or *accomplishment*.
The connection results from the preposition *mul* - מול for *opposite.*
The root *g-m-l*, with the prefixed *G*, would express the complex of relation to the *opposite* contained in *mul.*

Gimul - as *the deed*, *the accomplishment* - thus presents itself as the independent movement arising from being opposite, the *I-Thou relationship*.

Martin Buber illustrates this theme in his writing: *Urdistanz und Beziehung – primeval distance and relationship*
In German, this word-field is comparable with the relation of the word *gegen - against* and the terms *Begegnung - encounter* , *gegenüber – opposite* or *Gegenwart - presence*.

This implies an independent beginning. The camel stands for the way of this independent movement.

It points to the third between two - hence the number image for the three.
The importance of independence in faithfulness is complemented by the undemanding nature of the camel, enabling it to cover long distances without water in the desert; but also by its ability to smell water wells over long distances and to lead the traveler there,i.e. to guide him.
In its modest requirements it points to spiritual independence.
And to the autonomy of the person.

The metaphorical connection of the image of the camel with these contents has a long tradition in Judaism. It goes back to the story of courtship for Isaac, in which Rebekah proves to be the right bride, because she too draws water for the ten camels, which the matchmaker brings along, and also gives them drink. In the rabbinic interpretation the ten camels are associated with the ten commandments. The figure of the camel as a reminder in the story of the rich man, who cannot part with his possessions, also arises from this background.

Possession and complacency, property and enowning
Habe and *Behäbigkeit, Eigentum* and *Ereignis*

The German word *Behäbigkeit* comes from the verb *haben - to have*. It means *complacency, staidness*
The crucial element in the story of the camel, which passes through the eye of the needle rather than a rich man enters heaven is evidently the relation to possessions or property, to what belongs to man.

When, after Easter, in the story of the catch of fish at night, mentioning the 153 fish, to the images of camel and eye of the needle the *Nun* is added, it is worth asking what has changed in this relationship.

What is the relationship to the things of which we say that they belong to us?
In German the term for belonging comes from *hören – to hear, to listen*. To *belong* means *gehören*.

Is this connection characterized by the fact that they listen to us – *auf uns hören* - and therefore belong to us, are owned by us?
What is intrinsic to a person, his or her singularity also means that they have their own relationship to each other.

The etymology of the word *Ereignis – enowning, occurrence, event* is not considered to be related to the etymology of the words *eignen* or *Eigentum - owning* or *property*.

The word *Ereignis* comes from *Auge - eye.* In the original sense it means that

something has come to eye and is experienced with the eye.
Comparable to *hearing* in the sense of *gehören* here the seeing is referred to.

The adjective *eigen* – *own* or *peculiar* in linguistic history, on the other hand, is attributed to the Germanic *egen*, which means *to have, to own*, as in Old English *agan,* which became *own*.
The conversion of the initial sound *au* to *ei* in the case of *eräugen* and *ereignen* is, so the linguistic opinion, a false reference to the word family of *eigen*, resulting from dialectal blurring

However, one wonders if perhaps a more fundamental morphology applies than one which forms categories by word-historical attributions and lineages.

It is not without reason that we see the word *eye* in direct relation to identity. The German word *Augenblick* – literally: *eyelook,* meaning *moment,* is a synonym for the presence., *looking someone in the eye* means encountering him; it is also abstracted when we say, *to look danger In the eye*.

The spectrum of the initial vowel *au / ei* always seems to indicate a certain field of meaning. It addresses the existence coming out of nothing. The individual in relation to the surrounding. Like the land in the water.

For example in the case of *island*, Ger. *Eiland*, so in the name of *Jersey, Guernsey, Alderney,* etc., where the diphtong *ey* originally referred to an island, a land in the water.

Accordingly, the German word *Auge*, in English *eye*. Pupil and iris appear as an island in the white of the eyeball.

Similarly, the German word *Ei*, pronounced *I*, in English *egg.*
Although it belongs to the Semitic language family, Hebrew in this context has numerous similarities, e.g. in the word for *island*, - Hebrew *e* אי, as well as the word for *eye*, Hebrew *ayin* – עין.

Likewise the word for *One*, in German *Eins*, in Hebrew *echad* אחד.

Entering into existence from nothingness, the beginning, finds in Hebrew expression through the character of the first letter. The *Aleph* א, from which the Greek *Alpha* and subsequently the *A* of the Latin letter series derive, originally represents only the unvoiced initial sound with which each vowel begins when it is at the beginning of a word.

We identify the eye with the peculiarity, the ownness, thesingularity of a human being, the *Augenblick - moment* is synonymous with the presence.

The uniqueness or *ownness* of the individual does not arise through the distinction from the other - this is only a consequence - but because it is out of nothingness.

Hence the adequate initial sound in the word *Ereignis - enowning.* Implying his presence, that something is enowning to it and it is enowning.
The enowning is the relationship between the one who recognises and what is being recognized.

We possess the possession, the owned -
property is owning or propering to us.
While the notion of *possession* – German:
Besitz, includes *sessio* – *seat,* German:
Sitz, suggests a more passive relationship,
the notion of *owned* seems to imply a
dynamic, evolving, enowning relationship
between person and what comes toward –
the object.
The ability to enowning, to be a person,
means that things belong to man's own.
Nevertheless, this owning is not
possession.

Perhaps, in contrast to the concept of the
own and of the relation that is established
in it, the concept of possession refers to a
sessio, to *sitting*, to a tendency toward
staidness in relation to things.
To give one's possessions to the poor
would then be the recommendation to
change that relationship.
The concept of owning, in contrast to that
of possession, is more dynamic. It results
from the relationship to the object and is
defined by it.

In this sense, Hebrew has a linguistic peculiarity with which owning is expressed as an enowning.

Thus, the Hebrew language does not contain an adequate word for *to have*. The relation is articulated by the basic word of existence, *jesch-* יֵשׁ. Consequently the question: *Do you have a cup?* would literally be translated as: *Is you a cup?*

The existence-word *jesch-* יֵשׁ - *there is, it is*, has at the same time the meaning of identity or essence, *jeschut* יֵשׁוּת, as well as *existence* or *being* in general.

It is also part of the name *jeshua* - יֵשׁוּעָה, meaning *salvation.*

The question of possessions is thus posed in a new way.

Ownership as an expression of the person would then no longer be a possession in the sense of being occupied, but it would be an own which emerges from the enowning and becomes an enowning, it enowns in the enowning. Occurs in the occurring.

The German prefix *er* in the word *Ereignis* signifies the movement away from itself, out of itself; expressing the relationship with the other. It is comparable to the *en* in *encounter*. Hence the translation as *enowning.*

The Ereignis can be considered as a relationship. One's own gets related in an enowning.
The *Ereignis* is between I and Thou.

Occurrence is another term to translate the concept into English. It comes from Latin word *occurrere – going to meet, coming to view, encounter.*
It becomes apparent, when one says synonymously, *something has encountered* for *something occurred.*

If the concept of possession implies *sitting* or *occupying,* and thus the danger of staidness, inertia or immobility associated with such a conception of having, then the camel, as the animal of the path, stands for the commandment to be on the way, to stay on the way.

The biblical prohibition of the interest economy, the establishment of the *jubel*-year in which acquired land was returned and dependencies were resolved, and the further economic arrangements in the Mosaic directives are aimed at another form of having.

What belongs to the human being here is not a value abstracted from man per se but is related to and defined by the neediness of men.

A possession that is defined not by itself, but by the neediness of man, would thus become a social impulse.

It would no longer be static - not possession in the sense of occupation, but an own in the sense of the enowning.
It would be an expression of the spirit.
Substance of the enowning.

Man

This is the new thing to which *Nun*, the *fish* hints, when it is added to camel und eye of a needle in middle of the number of the 153. By taking in the *I Am*, the individual becomes a person.
He becomes able to enown. Only in this way can things be freed from stagnation - and can become a *new earth*.

And then the camel will be able to go through the eye of the needle.

It makes sense here that in the Hebrew word for *person / human - anosch -* אנוש, in the plural a*neschim -* אנשים, the word *I - ani -* אני. is included.
Humans are the ones, who can say *I.*

With the relationship of the 153 fish to the parable of Camel and eye of a needle , other features of the description of the nightly catch of fish gain a response-like importance.

Those who had heard the parable of the camel which passes through the eye of a needle, rather than a rich man enters the

kingdom of heaven, asked scared, who
can be saved at all

The answer Jesus gave them at that time,
*What is impossible with man, is possible
with God*, is answered again here, after
the resurrection, by pointing out the great
number of fish.
And that even though there were so many,
the net was not torn.

***

Notes

Hebrew Basis of the Gospels

A study of the Gospels by means of the Hebrew etymology and with the help of the Gematria can, according to the principles of their system, at first only be devoted to the Hebrew terms

In the Greek texts of the Gospels, these are the original Hebrew or Aramaic forms of names and place names. Moreover, a Hebrew reference to all figures is to be assumed.

Individual words and passages, especially in the repetition of direct speech, may also be inferred from Hebrew, since the Greek traditions reflect speeches and discussions conducted in Judea-Aramaic and Hebrew.

It is to be assumed that Hebrew, in addition to the supra-regional Aramaic and the Greek of the coastal regions, was still spoken in everyday life in the interior of the country, similar to the frequent coexistence of regional language, dialect and high-level language.

Certainly, as Martin Buber points out, Hebrew was spoken in the teachings and religious dialogues of the time of Jesus - and not only in the liturgy.

However, as shown by the above contexts, a fundamental reference to Hebrew beyond the narrative content can be presupposed in the writing of the Gospels.

The authors of the Gospels were Jews, they spoke and thought in Hebrew, the peculiarity of Hebrew etymology was self-evident to them.

In any case, Hebrew original texts are to be presupposed. The idea that in the Jewish-Christian communities in the interior of the country, in Jerusalem, Judea, Samaria and Galilee, text written in Greek were read, is highly unrealistic. The existence of Hebrew Christian writings does not only become apparent in references of some early Christian theologists, like Hieronymus or Euseb or in puns, which, like the one described here, are only revealed in Hebrew, but also in a first-century Talmudic passage, which discusses the question of how to deal with the books of the Jewish Christians, the *minim*, regarding the commandment to save Hebrew texts in a fire.

Money

In the Torah, the directive is pronounced that money should not be made into a commodity, that is, not to pursue an interest-yielding economy:

If any of your people become poor and unable to support themselves, you must help them, just as you are supposed to help the foreigner or sojourner who live among you. Don't take advantage of them by charging any kind of interest or selling them food for profit. Lev. 25, 35-37

Also, the other Mosaic rules on property and the economy, such as the periodic abolition of all dependencies and mismatches in the fiftieth year, are a guide to understanding property and currency as a means of social circulation and impulsation.

Possession should be determined by the neediness of man.
If it is isolated and neutralized, it develops an absolute nature. It becomes what the word *mammon* means.

As a means of economic interaction – of trade - it then assumes the meaning of a yardstick. Thus, in consequence, it approaches man as a determining factor.

In this way, the rules of trade and economy develop their own momentum and serve no longer as means of social action, but determine it.

When possession is perceived as a value in itself, it means that the money is relieved of its intermediary function, taken out of circulation, and converted

into possession. It is then itself a commodity, which is traded in the economy of interest rates and stock markets and is, in turn, money-increasing and profitable.
One of the results is an increase in unrelated money, with no real efficiency and no real economic value.

Another is the emergence of power constellations which are ends in themselves – corresponding to the subjectless and objectless money, which itself became commodity – and which are therefore at the same time non- personal, anonymous and totalitarian.

Aristotle identified this process and justified his refusal:
As this is so, usury is most reasonably hated, because its gain comes from money itself and not from that for the sake of which money was invented. For money was brought into existence for the purpose of exchange, but interest increases the amount of the money itself (and this is the actual origin of the Greek word: offspring resembles parent, and interest is money born of money) ;

consequently this form of the business of getting wealth is of all forms the most contrary to nature.

The Greek word τόκῳ - *toko* is derived from something that is *born*. For Aristotle, the unnaturalness of interest is based on the fact that money is labelled with the quality of being alive, namely that capital multiplies like a herd in which young are born.
This is similar to the modern euphemism to have *money work*; likewise capital and interest are compared with a *hen laying eggs*.

In ancient times, independent movement was considered the essential criterion of life. This is why Aristotle sees pseudo-growth in the interest-rate economy. Money is begotten from the relationship to the commodity. But when money is produced by money, when it becomes itself a commodity, it can no longer serve the exchange of commodities.

The establishment of money as a means of exchanging goods requires a countervalue to goods and services in a corresponding amount of money supply within the community. In order to fulfil its task of economic communication, this money must remain in flux.

If a city dams up the water on the upper reaches of a river and then sells it against interest to the lower reaches, there are good reasons for objections.
But the situation is similar to stemming the flow of money and thus turning money itself into a commodity.

It contradicts its purpose when it is hoarded or, in the analogy of the river, dammed to sell it profitably.
The resulting added value would have no equivalent and no relation to a good or service. But as it is given a value, it can only fill that void with a steady devaluation of the real relationship between performance and money.

In the Mosaic rules regarding commercial transactions, the question of interest is discussed several times.
In one passage the prohibition seems to be categorical:

The *brother as well as the stranger* should be supported and it is forbidden to take interest from him. Lev. 25, 35-37

In another passage, with regard to the taking of land in Canaan, the prohibition of interest only applies to the brother but interest may be imposed on the foreigner: *Unto a foreigner thou mayest lend upon interest; but unto thy brother thou shalt not lend upon interest.* 5.Mose 23,20

The original Hebrew text uses two different terms. In the first case, *ger* – גֵּר the stranger living in the country, and in the second *nochri* - נָכְרִי, the foreigner from abroad.

The contradiction is clarified when the instruction is related to an existing community, in which performance, commodity and money form a corresponding relationship.

In the economic cycle of this polity, the taking of interest would mean an increase in money without equivalent value and disrupt the healthy circulation. The poor would become poorer without any guilt,

and the rich would become richer without
merit.

To prevent this is the purpose of the
interest ban.
Therefore, among the members of the
economic community, whether natives or
immigrants, the prohibition of interest
shall apply.

If, however, an amount of money would be
lent from the commonwealth to the
members of another community, without
benefit for the first commonwealth, that
monetary value would be lacking in their
economic cycle.

This would mean a similar but reversed
disruption of the relation of value and
money. The amount of money no longer
corresponds to the product range. Also for
the other community whose members
borrowed the amount, a damage would be
caused by the emergence of a foreign
money quantity because there is no
equivalent value.

The prohibition of interest apparently
differentiates between the movement of

money within a community and between several separate and independent communities.

It obviously takes into account whether money transactions between the members of a trade association or members of different, separate and independent associations are concerned.

It distinguishes between the neighborly stranger who belongs to the same trade association and the stranger who belongs to a different, independent association. Within the associations, the taking of interest is prohibited, whereas, under certain circumstances, it is allowed between the associations in order to avoid an imbalance in the ratio of goods and money within the individual association.

What about today's globalized trade, in which the economic independence of individual associations can no longer exist?

Although there are different countries and political systems, a global economic structure, which affects all associations,

economically represents a uniform community.
Interest in this case means, as in the association of the Mosaic instructions, the production of money without equivalent value.

It is prohibited in Leviticus because money loses its quality of mediation and because, as a result, the last in the chain of interest and price increases, who can no longer pass on their additional costs to anyone, are deprived.

A trade in which money becomes a commodity or, as in the stock market, the increase in value itself is the cause of the increase in value, makes the gap between the haves and the have-nots unbridgeable and inevitably leads to the collapse of the economic cycle.

As regards the purchase of shares, when an investor buys a share in an economic initiative, the situation is different. Here his money has a real countervalue. If the company bears fruit, his share increases in proportion to the growing real value.

If the company fails, he loses his money. Profit and loss are borne by him. A steadily growing, non-cash value, as in the case of interest, does not arise.

Mutual relationship between the text of John and those of the other three evangelists

One characteristic of 153 is that its cross sum, nine, multiplied by the starting number seventeen, again yields one hundred and fifty-three.
Strangely enough, the seventeen has this in common only with its prime twin, the nineteen. (whose addition series is 190, i.e. the cross sum 10 multiplied by 19).

From this numerical relationship of the seventeen, the juxtaposition of the other three Gospels with that of John reveals a reciprocal relation: Not only the text of John with the number of 153 fish is linked to the story of camel and eye of the needle, but the three other Gospels also refer to the nocturnal fish catch in the text of John when viewed together.

This when, conspicuously, the word good, טוב - *tov*, which is common to all three descriptions is mentioned three times.

The word, yielding seventeen when read as a number, is spoken three times at the beginning of the dialogue between Jesus and the rich man in all three gospels. Once on the part of the rich man and twice in the answer from Jesus. The answer can be considered as one of the passages in the New Testament where Jesus expresses who he is. Here, by pronouncing the consequence of the salutation - *What do you call me good, no one is good but one, God*.

Due to the conspicuously matching, three times mention of the *tov* - טוב in all three descriptions, the result is nine times the numerical value of seventeen. That equals one hundred and fifty-three. The other three Gospels would then, quasi united, in the context of the parable of camel and eye of the neelde mention the hidden numerical value of hundred-fifty-three - and as such also refer to the fish catch after resurrection in the text of John.

A similar relationship in terms of the numerical value of the word tov can be seen in the story of the Flood.

Here, at the new beginning after the flood, when the waters began to sink again, it is mentioned that it was the seventeenth day of the seventh month, when Noah's Ark touched down on Mount Ararat. 1. Moses, 8,4

The numbers seem to refer to Genesis in the sense of a new beginning, where it is said seven times how God, looking at his works, *saw that it was good*, and thus the word *tov* with the numerical value of the seventeen is used seven times.

Noteworthy in this context is Augustine's reference to the seventeenth verse of the seventeenth psalm.
(According to the original count in Tanach and Septuagint, later by dividing the 9th Psalm in a 9th and 10th Psalm, the 17th is denoted as the 18th psalm).

There, in Psalm 17, verse 17 it reads:
He stretched out his hand, reaching for me, pulling me out of the great waters.

The theme of pulling out is also the etymological basis of the name Moses, Moscheh, who is both the one who is pulled out from the water and the one who pulls out (M. Buber), who draws the people out of bondage.

Another mathematical feature is the *measure of the fish* attributed to Archimedes.

A measurement ratio resulting from two overlapping circles of equal size, where the circle line of one leads through the centre of the other.

The cut surface results in the shape of a mandorla. The Gothic arch is also based on this figure.

If one connects the outer points of the two circle lines by a straight line, the cut surface receives a tail fin and forms the figure of a fish.

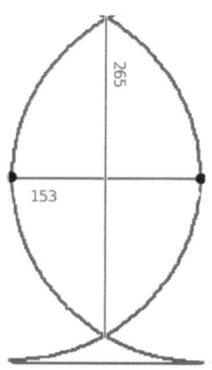

Archimedes formulated the ratio between the radius of the circles and the distance between the two points of intersection as 153 to 265. The decimal number of this ratio, the number 1,732, yields the root of the number three.

Nun as a word for the presence

In the word field of the concept of presence, a remarkable significance can be observed with which a content appears beyond language borders and epochs in similar or identical words.
Like in the case of an Aquinas translation into German, where it is said that *Christ is the eternal Now - Christus ist das ewige Nun Nun.*
The German word *Nun*, in the Old High German *Nu*, is like the English *Now*, related to the Greek *Nyn - Now*. The Greek consonant *Ny* goes back to the Semitic letter *Nun*, the *y* to the Semitic *vav*. In this respect, the Greek *Nyn* represents an immediate takeover of the Hebrew-Aramaic letter name *Nun*, with the meaning of the fish.

The tetragram and the instruction to charity

The tetragram, the four-letter name of God, that God announces to Moses from out of the burning bush, is explained by Martin Buber as *the basic word of the person* - as the *I-Thou.*

Since the Babylonian exile the Holy Name has been considered as ineffable in Judaism.
Therefore, when reciting the Scripture the term *Adonai*, Hebrew: *my Lord*, is chosen instead.

In the early days of the Christian translations of the Old Testament, the transcript simply took over the Hebrew letters of the tetragram.
When reciting a Greek edition people proceeded as in the Jewish tradition and pronounced *Adonai* or the corresponding Greek *Kyrios.*

When this context was no longer present in the course of the further spread of the Scripture, the written tetragram was replaced by a written *Kyrios*.

This rule was adopted in further translations, so that in Luther's Bible translation, the German *Herr – Lord* is used wherever the original Hebrew text mentioned the four-letter name of God. This solution sometimes led to a significant loss of meaning.

This is why Martin Buber used the personal pronouns, *I, Thou, He* in his transmission of Scripture instead of the name of God - which he understands as the basic word of the person.

The conclusiveness of this interpretation is proved by a translation of the commandment of charity into German, elaborated by Naftali Herz Wessely in the 19th century and adopted by many Jewish and Christian translators.
The conventional form reads:
Thou shalt love thy neighbour as thyself.

However, the phrase *as thyself - kamocha* - can be transferred more accurately with:
(he is) like you.
The translation by Wessely, based on the comparison with similar passages, is therefore:

Thou shall love your neighbour, for he is like thou - I am the Lord. 3.Moses 19:18 and 19:34

In this translation of the instruction, the other human is perceived as an *I-being - anosch -*, as a person *like thou.*

Thus, the statement goes beyond the more reflective nature of the conventional translation and provides an essential directive to the relationship.

This instruction by Jesus is emphasized in Matt. 22, 35-40, together with the directive of the love for God, as one of the two most important instructions that stand above all others.When a scribe asked him which was the chief commandment in the Torah, Jesus answered him by quoting these two commandments from the Torah and equating them:

Thou shalt love the Lord thy God with thy whole heart and with thy whole soul and with thy whole mind and with thy whole strength. 5. Mose 6,5

This is the first commandment. And the second is like unto it: Thou shalt love thy neighbor for he is like thou. 3.Mose 19,18. On these two commandments dependeth the whole law and the prophets.

In the Tanach, in 3 Moses 19:18, the statement concludes with the mention of the Tetragram: *I am* יהוה .

For this reason, Buber and Rosenzweig decided to translate: *Halte lieb deinen Genossen, dir gleich. ICH bins - Love your neighbor, like thou. It's me.*

What can be recognized is the agreement with another essential statement of Jesus: *What you have done to the least of my brothers you have done to me.* Math., 25:40

Name and designation

The four-letter name of God, which God announces to Moses at the sight of the burning bush, is regarded as sacred in Judaism.
Unlike the *Name of God* so described, the biblical *Elohim* with which Genesis begins is not mentioned as the *Name of God*.

This Hebrew title *Elohim* forms a plural by the ending *im*. In view of the emphasis on the uniqueness of God in Judaism, this is explained by the fact that this word is not meant to designate God in his incomprehensibility/ unknowability, but the totality of the powers of God working in creation (Rashi).
It is understood as an approximate designation.

For Jewish theology the awe and transcendence towards the incomprehensible unity of God lies precisely in the application of the plural.

This does not apply for the tetragram. It is expressly proclaimed to Moses from out of the burning bush as the eternal name of God.

The *Ejeh Asher Ejeh - I-Am-The-I-Am* is therefore not to be understood as a designation or title.

It is the self-expression of the unfathomable deity that is becoming present, the principle of identity that can only be addressed in immediate speech – with *thou*.

The *Shin* in the name of *Yehoshua*

The letters of the Tetragram also appear
in the name of Jesus of Nazareth,
Yehoshua - יהושע.
But here, instead of the final second *He* - ה
of the Tetragram - יהוה, there is a *Shin* – ש.

In the tradition of the Hebrew language,
the letter *Shin* is associated with the
image of the human teeth - *Shinaim*.

The intake and mastication of food, which
happens with the teeth, thus stands -
according to the meaning of the letter-
image - for the human ability to judge and
to make decisions.

A similar metaphor of teeth can be found
in the Chinese *Book of Changes*, the
I Ging.
There, the 21th oracle of *biting through*
indicates the specific character of a
decision-making process in its
consequence. The variants of the oracle
read *it bites through soft meat, bites on
cartilage meat*, or *bites on old dried meat.*
(R. Wilhelm)

The *Shin* is sometimes pronounced in Hebrew also as *Ssin*, as an unvoiced *S*, which is distinguished accordingly in the later punctuation of Hebrew script.

There is a special story in the Bible associated with this different pronunciation of the Shin that decided the fate of the people of the tribe of Ephraim . Judges 12: 4-6

This was preceded by a border conflict. The Ammonites had invaded the land of the twelve tribes, and the inhabitants of Gilead near the border thereupon asked their allies, the Ephraimites, for assistance.
But they refused to to help so that the Gileadites fought the war alone and finally defeated the Ammonites.
Thereafter, however, the Ephraimites threatened the leader of Gilead, Jeftach, and claimed a share of the war booty.
Jeftach gathered his people and successfully fought against the Ephraimites who fled towards the River Jordan.

The people of Gilead now occupied the fords of the Jordan. Ephraimite refugees who wanted to cross the Jordan to get to the other shore had to say the word *Shiboleth* - the Hebrew word for *ear of wheat,* also for *flow* or *stream.* As like the ear of wheat seems like an image of a flow.

Those who could not pronounce it correctly, but were only able to say *Siboleth,* a peculiarity of the Ephraimites, were recognized and killed because they had previously denied their help in the fight against the Ammonites, but afterwards had attacked the people of Gilead to get the spoils of war.

Their inability to pronounce the *Shin* in *Shiboleth* seems to stand for the stinginess and lack of helpfulness of the Ephraimites. The character of flowing appears in the *Sh,* not in the *S.*

The word *Shiboleth* became a concept beyond its biblical context because of this destiny of the Ephraimites; *Shiboleth* is a proverbial synonym for a fate-determining decision.

Martin Buber calls the *"I"* the *shiboleth of this time*. (Martin Buber, *I and Thou*)
Therefore, the meaning of the *Shin* in the sense of being in opposition, contains the separation into I and Thow - the precondition of the relationship and thus of the decision.
Thus, the *Shin* also stands for presence, for being present.

For Christian experts of Hebrew mysticism, the Shin in the name of Jesus was the added fifth consonant of the four-letter name of God, which had been made known to Moses by the burning bush.
For the Christian representatives of Kabbalah - such as John Reuchlin and Agrippa von Nettesheim - the *Shin* in *Yehoshua* means the fulfilment of the name of God. In it the Incarnation of Him who had manifested Himself in the tetragram is expressed. The *Shin* stands for his presence, his coming-down into time.

Tsippor Nefesh, נ - the *Nun*

In Jewish mysticism, the Hebrew letter *Nun* - נ stands for the individuation of man, for the individual in time. The *Nun* is also called *Tsipor Nefesh* צפור נפש, the *Soul Bird*.

Tsippor Nefesh is like the wit. Like the wave, the wit comes out of the *w*, out of the water. The wave goes back into the water but the wit becomes uniqueness and flies.

The wit flies, and if it has to be explained, it is trapped. An explained joke is no joke anymore.

Nisht geshteugen, nisht gefleugen – Not risen up, not flown is a Yiddish saying, about a thing that is neither one thing nor another.
Tsipor Nefesh is the uniqueness of the individual human being, which distinguishes him from all others.

About which it is said in Psalm: *Deliver my soul from the sword, my one and only, from the power of dog.* Psalm 22:20
The hebrew word in the original text is *ichidit* - יחידת, coming from *achad*- אחד - *one*, meaning *only one, the identity, the unique,* offen translated as *my darling* or *my precious life.*
The freedom of its essence.

***